Trans-Siberian Orchestra
Night Castle

Story and lyrics by Paul O'Neill

CONTENTS

Night Castle: *The Story* 2	Moonlight and Madness 134
Night Enchanted 25	Time Floats On 144
Childhood Dreams 36	Epiphany 149
Sparks 41	Bach Lullaby 168
The Mountain 53	Father, Son & Holy Ghost 169
Night Castle 63	Remnants of a Lullaby 181
The Safest Way Into Tomorrow 70	The Safest Way Into Tomorrow (Reprise) 187
Mozart and Memories 77	Embers 189
Another Way You Can Die 88	Child of the Night 195
Toccata-Carpimus Noctem 96	Believe 203
The Lion's Roar 102	Nutrocker 213
Dreams We Conceive 108	Carmina Burana 224
Mother and Son 19	Tracers 231
There Was a Life 117	

WWW.TRANS-SIBERIAN.COM

Produced by
Alfred Music Publishing Co., Inc.
P.O. Box 10003
Van Nuys, CA 91410-0003
alfred.com

Printed in USA.

No part of this book shall be reproduced, arranged, adapted, recorded, publicly performed, stored in a retrieval system, or transmitted by any means without written permission from the publisher. In order to comply with copyright laws, please apply for such written permission and/or license by contacting the publisher at alfred.com/permissions.

ISBN-10: 0-7390-8622-7
ISBN-13: 978-0-7390-8622-3

© Cover and interior art: Greg Hildebrandt
www.spiderwebart.com
Album art direction and design: David J. Harrigan

In the seventh year of her life, a young girl was nearing the end of her seventh summer, at a beach house that her grandfather had built on the Pacific Ocean, long before she was born. It was a beautiful but simple house, constructed high atop the dunes, overlooking a seemingly endless stretch of pristine, sandy beach. She believed that her grandfather must have been the wisest of men to have procured such a perfect spot. It was far enough away from the water to be perfectly safe from the crashing waves of the largest storms, when the ocean was at its most mischievous, but close enough that she could still hear the quietest of breakers, on the calmest of nights as they gently lulled her to sleep.

Night Enchanted
(Page 25)

It was the final night of the season and she knew that tomorrow she would be returning home. So, she snuck out of bed, to sit out on her balcony and gaze at the stars as they appeared one at a time or occasionally in clusters. She was happily lost in her own little world, savoring the last moments of summer, when she noticed what seemed like a swarm of fireflies, playfully flying over the crashing waves. Looking downward, she saw that a man had gathered a large pile of driftwood, dried reeds and rushes and was igniting it with a handheld Zippo lighter. As the dried rushes caught fire, the summer breezes fanned the flames until even the largest logs and planks were burning brightly. Occasionally, one of the bigger pieces of wood would fall, causing an explosion of sparks to be thrown high into the night air, where the wind was waiting to carry them out over the ocean waters.

As the bonfire grew in intensity, it illuminated a large sandcastle that the man had obviously been working on for a considerable time. Once he was satisfied that the bonfire was well established, he returned to finishing his edifice of sand. Now, most children are fascinated by bonfires, sandcastles and of course staying up late when one should be asleep and this combination of all three was proving near irresistible. Correction, make that irresistible. For a moment, she pondered obtaining parental permission to go down to look at this castle, but asking meant risking the most universal of adult replies, a stern and emphatically delivered, "No!" So, she decided to sneak out on her own. Carefully climbing over the balcony railing, she quietly crept down the stairs and across the beach to examine this wonderment close-up.

Childhood Dreams
(Page 36)

As she neared the bonfire, she could see that the individual, who was casting such a large shadow when silhouetted against the fire, was in reality, a thin, but muscular man with shoulder length hair. He was wearing a faded black t-shirt with the initials for New York City printed boldly on the front in big block letters. The castle he was building was even more magical than she could have imagined when she viewed it from a distance. It had large thick walls, surrounded by a deep moat and numerous towers. He had hollowed out a little room inside the tallest tower and had placed a small tea candle inside, so that the room glowed with an orange light from within.

Now, all this time, she was quite certain that he was completely unaware of her presence, until quite unexpectedly, the man, who now had his back to her asked, "Would you like to help?"

Surprised, that he was somehow aware of her presence, she stepped out from the darkness and replied, "What can I do?"

"Well, the main gate still needs a drawbridge and I think that small piece of wood under your right foot would fit perfectly."

She looked down and said, "I'm sorry sir, but there is only sand under my feet."

"Ahh, yes," he answered without looking up from the rampart upon which he was putting the final touches, "but what lies beneath that sand?"

Wiggling her toes in the sand under her feet, she was delighted to discover a small weathered rectangular plank, which she could tell at first glance would fit perfectly into the main gate leading across the moat. Picking it up, she ran over and handed it to the gentleman, a smile beaming from her face. Returning her smile, he took the small plank and placed it across the moat leading to the front gate.

Together, they stepped back to look at the now completed castle. The man noticed that parts of the wall had been dried out slightly by the heat from the fire, and sitting down, started

to scoop handfuls of water from the moat to re-moisten the sand before it crumbled. The child, quickly joined him and within moments they had repaired all the damage.

As the unlikely pair sat back, they gazed in satisfaction at their creation now back-lit by the bonfire and enchanted by the sparks that seemed to hesitate over it, as if in homage, as they flew by on their way to the sea.

"Do you live near here?" the child inquired of her newfound friend.

"No, I actually live quite far away, but I come to the ocean shores as often as possible," he replied.

"Why?"

"Well, I want to visit all the places on earth, which of course is impossible, especially for a person with limited financial resources. But a friend I once had, told me that when you touch the ocean, you touch the entire world. For the oceans touch the entire earth. Every continent, every island, large and small, every inlet and peninsula and through all the rivers and streams that empty into these oceans, they also reach deep into the largest bodies of land." The man then picked up a handful of water and reaching out placed it in the hand of the child. "Imagine how many drops are in just this small handful of water. Now, only a short while ago, one of those drops was on the shore of the Baltic Sea, and that one was in the Sea of Japan and the one next to it came from atop the Andes Mountains, down the Maranon and Amazon Rivers, across Peru and Brazil, until it reached the Atlantic Ocean."

"And right there," he said pointing to a corner of her hand, "is one of my favorites, for it has taken the longest journey. It originally came from the eyes of the Egyptian Queen, Cleopatra, as she held her child from Julius Caesar and realized that she would never see the great Roman leader again. It fell from her eye, down her cheek and into the Nile where it passed the Temples of Memphis and Luxor, the Pyramids of Giza and the ever-patient gaze of the Great Sphinx before entering the Mediterranean. From there, it visited the harbors of Alexandria, Athens and Rome before slipping through the Straits of Gibraltar, where it continued its journey for over two millennium, before it ended up here, in your hands."

"Really?" she asked.

"What do you think?" he countered.

"It might be," she replied hopefully.

"I think so too."

For a moment, the child pondered all these new and wondrous facts that had just been revealed to her about that single drop of water, and then, she very carefully, reverently, placed that handful of water back into the tip of the next wave that washed up at their feet and said, "This way someone else might hold it one day. Your friend must have been a very smart man."

"He was."

"How did you meet him?"

"That, my young friend, is a long story."

"I love stories," she eagerly replied.

"Well, it began many years ago."

"How long?" she queried.

"Before you were even born."

"Wow!" she said, her forehead wrinkled in contemplation, "That is a long time. Were you kids together?"

"No, my earliest memory of his life was when he was a newly commissioned army lieutenant, on 42nd Street in New York City, on the night that he first met the young lady he would marry."

"Is 42nd Street a park?" she asked in all earnestness.

The question was so unexpected, that it momentarily threw the gentleman off. He tried to gather his thoughts as to how he could describe to a child, the Times Square area of New York City, at a time when it was known as "Hell's Kitchen," an area where the lost souls, drug addicts, winos, criminals and the other unwanted offspring of humanity, had created a little, surrealistic, neon lit, Oz. A sanctuary for the hopeless and the hunted, right in the middle of the greatest city on earth, and how it was in this environment, the last place his friend ever would have predicted, that the Lieutenant first saw and fell in love with his future wife.

In the beginning, he struggled to put together the words, but eventually he found them flowing easier and easier about the moment the couple's eyes first met from a distance. They were walking towards each other, the Lieutenant from the Port Authority on 42nd Street and Eighth Avenue and she from the library on 42nd Street and Fifth Avenue. How in the early evening, on that crowded street, they both looked away with embarrassment, yet they both slowed their pace. How when they were only twenty feet apart, even the drug dealers and street walkers could see that the soldier so badly wanted to introduce himself to this beautiful young lady, but how could he on this criminally infested street? But then she stopped and pretended to look in a store window and he did the same as they glanced at each other's reflections in the glass. When she finally turned and started to walk again, he realized that if he missed this opportunity he would regret it for the rest of his life. So, just as she was about to pass him by, he introduced himself and she instantly returned the gesture. After some small talk, they agreed to meet the next afternoon for lunch. She wrote down the phone number of his hotel and then she continued on her way home. After watching her disappear into the crowd, the Lieutenant started back towards his hotel. Now, unbeknownst to my friend, a drug dealer who had been watching the entire scene from across the street walked up to him and said, 'Man, what is your problem soldier? I thought you were never going to ask her out!'

'Excuse me?' The Lieutenant asked.

'I was watching you two, from the minute I saw that girl's eyes meet yours and a blind man could tell you were meant to be together. But it was near torture waiting for you to say something. For a minute I was nearly convinced you were going to let that piece of magic slip right out of your life, but in the end you came through.'

'What exactly did you think you saw?' The Lieutenant countered, in a slightly bemused voice.

"On this street, my kingdom, my world, I see everything," the dealer replied. "I saw you, I saw her, I saw what could be and I saw sparks!"

Sparks
(Page 41)

The Lieutenant found this drug dealer fascinating. Here was a man who could probably barely write his own name, but had spent so much of his life scanning the faces on that street for potential customers, that he could tell in an instant if they were on their way to work, school or home, or if they were looking for an illicit substance and what that illicit substance was. This individual was so amoral that he would sell anyone enough heroin to kill themselves without a second thought, but somehow he wanted to see

these two complete strangers meet and have a happy ending. The Lieutenant and the drug dealer spoke for a while, the dealer telling him that he was positive the young lady would call him back and the officer promising that if she did, he would send the dealer a postcard from Saigon. A short while later, they parted ways as the drug dealer went back across the street and the Lieutenant headed to his hotel with the dealer's address in his wallet and the hope that one day he would be mailing that postcard from Saigon in Vietnam.

And the dealer was to be proven right, for despite all the Lieutenant's fears that she might have second thoughts and never call, at exactly noon, the phone rang and by that night they were married.

"I love weddings! Did they have a flower girl?"

"I don't think so."

"Was it a big wedding?"

"No, remember I said they got married the day after they met. I believe it was at the city hall."

"Really? The next day? How did they know they were in love?"

"The minute they saw each others' eyes there was magic."

"Why didn't they wait so that their friends and family could have been there?"

"Well, you see little one, my friend was in the army, and not just the regular army, but a division of the army that is known as Special Forces. That is the most difficult part of any military unit to join, the part with the hardest of training. Training that is so tough that most men give up before completing it. But my friend completed the entire course and shortly after his graduation was assigned as an officer to a unit stationed in Europe. He was only in New York City for two days before he was to fly overseas and so that is why they got married so quickly. The day after the wedding, she drove him to JFK Airport for the flight that would take him to his army unit at their base in Europe."

"Couldn't she go to Europe too?"

"Normally, yes, but he knew that he was only to be in Europe for a short while before they would be deployed to fight in Southeast Asia. Their mission was to help the people of a country called Cambodia fight against a group known as the Khmer Rouge, a communist backed guerrilla army who were trying to take over the country. The night before they were to depart, my friend's entire unit was given a final night's leave. Being young of course, they went in search of the nearest bar, which happened to be in a little fishing town not too far from their base. Once there, my friend got fairly inebriated."

"What is inebriated?" the girl asked struggling to pronounce the unfamiliar word.

"Hmmm," the man said while stroking his chin thoughtfully, "He became a little too intoxicated."

The child still looked confused.

"How can I explain? Let us just say that he consumed too many beverages with an unusually high alcoholic content that temporarily impaired his better judgment."

"Oh!" the child exclaimed, "He got drunk!"

"Very astute for such a small child," the man chuckled.

The child beamed proudly at the compliment as he continued his story. "Now this… getting drunk is not the brightest of ideas, but even very wise men have been known to do it on occasion. As the evening wore on, my friend eventually became separated from his fellow soldiers. Without any money to get a taxi back to the base he found himself wandering down the wharf, where he saw a small, two man fishing boat tied to a dock. Its sails were down and neatly folded with the nets at the bottom of the boat. Deciding that the owner probably would not mind if he waited there 'til morning when a bus could get him back to his unit, he got in the boat, laid down on the sails and within minutes had fallen asleep to the gentle rocking of the small vessel.

Suddenly, my friend was awakened by a small bump. Rousing himself from his slumber, he looked around and quickly realized that the boat was no longer tied to the dock. Somehow, while he was sleeping, it must have slipped loose of its mooring. The bump that had awakened him was the boat drifting ashore on a small stretch of beach, surrounded by tall sheer cliffs. He could see no signs of life and the only light was coming from the cloudless night sky.

Now, he was really starting to worry. He had no idea where he was, let alone how to get back to where he should be. He worried that if he was not at his base by morning, he would officially be declared away without leave, possibly even charged with desertion. If he could not find his way back to civilization, his family would not know what had happened to him. No one would have any idea where to look for him and his worst fear was that some might think that he had deserted his fellow soldiers, right before they were to go into combat.

Desperately, he looked about for any signs of life but all he could see was sand, cliffs and the ocean. Then, as he turned his gaze upwards to see if there was a possible way to scale the cliffs, he saw an unusual but welcome sight. Set high atop the rocks, silhouetted in the light of that evening's full moon, was an enormous medieval castle. It was a fascinating collection of walls and buildings, ramparts and towers but the sight he found the most fascinating was the orange glow of a light emanating from the highest window, in the highest tower.

Rationalizing, that where there was light, there must be people, and also that whoever had built the castle, must have arranged a way to get to it from the beach, he slowly started to search along the cliff's bottom edge. After walking only several yards, he noticed hidden in the dimness, a series of steps cut into the rock leading upward."

"What did he do?" the child inquired eagerly.

"Well, what would you have done?" the man countered.

"I would have climbed up those stairs!"

"Amazing, because that's exactly what he did."

The Mountain
(Page 53)

The closer he got to the castle, the more magical it seemed. The walls appeared more massive, the towers more mysterious. When he finally reached the top, he saw the castle's main gate. It had two large stone gargoyles set in the wall above it, keeping silent vigil over this hidden kingdom but more importantly he noticed its large drawbridge was lowered, allowing him to easily enter its courtyard. Once again, scanning the skyline, he located the lit room and made a mental note as to its location and then started to try to discover a way to reach it. After trying several doors, he located one that was slightly ajar and with a gentle tug it slowly creaked open on its rusty hinges. Upon entering, he found himself within a great hall. It was a large, cavernous room, with a high vaulted ceiling supported by giant stone pillars. Directly across from the entrance, above a wooden throne on a raised platform, moonlight streamed through a large circular window that was missing most of its glass. Large arched windows, bereft of all glass, were set high in the walls on either side of the room, allowing him to clearly see the stars outside as well as a view of the lit tower room, so tantalizingly close, but still so far.

Unexpectedly, he saw the figure of a snow-white bird glide through one of the windows and alight on a wrought iron torch holder mounted into the stone masonry. As he looked closer, he realized that the bird was a falcon. The bird momentarily gazed at him and then once more took to flight. With an airborne dancer's ease, the falcon flew to the very top of the vaulted ceiling, before arcing back down. Her trajectory had the bird flying so close to my friend that he could feel the wind from her wings as she turned and flew towards an old tapestry hanging on a distant wall. There the bird suddenly disappeared. Running over to the area, my friend quickly discovered that at the spot where the falcon had vanished from sight, the tapestry had a fairly large tear and the remaining tapestry concealed nearly all of an entrance to an upwardly winding staircase.

Following the bird as quickly as he could, it was all he could do to keep her in sight as she flew up various stairways, down halls both long and short, through rooms both large and small. Some of the rooms contained sculptures and paintings, some ancient weapons of every type, others strange but oddly familiar mechanical devices and one that was filled with countless timepieces and clocks. Several of the timepieces were still ticking. He was so fascinated by this, that only the fear of losing sight of his swift winged guide prevented him from stopping to take a closer look. His instinct to not slow down proved correct as he nearly missed seeing the falcon fly through an open door that led to a series of sharply winding, extremely steep steps. He reached the top of the stairs just in time to see the falcon fly through an open arched doorway. Instantly, he realized that this was the room that he had been seeking. He could clearly see that the orange light he had observed from outside was emanating from a large ornately carved fireplace. The fire was happily consuming a healthy supply of logs and in return was generously spilling out its warmth and light to all.

Night Castle
(Page 63)

Cautiously entering, it took him several moments to take in all that appeared before him. The room was large and circular, lined with overstuffed bookcases. Scattered about the room were piles of manuscripts, antique scientific devices, compasses, hourglasses and ancient maps. Overfilled trunks gave enticing hints as to their contents. Jewels and gold coins were scattered about on various tables as casually as dust and empty ink bottles. Across the room, sitting at a large carved oak desk, was an old man with long white hair wearing a red medieval cloak who seemed entirely engrossed in what he was writing. Afraid of scaring the older man, my friend stood there silently, waiting for the chance to announce his presence. When the old man finished what he was writing, he picked up the piece of paper and reaching his hand out the open window before him, released the paper to a waiting breeze, which took hold of it and caressed it gently before helping the missive float away into the night.

Before the completed page was even out of sight the old man was starting on another. The Lieutenant, realizing that he might not have a better chance to alert the castle's lone resident of his presence without startling him, softly cleared his throat and in the most non-threatening voice he could muster, said, 'Excuse me sir, I don't mean to intrude but it seems that I'm lost.'

However, the old man was not startled. He didn't even look up from his writing as he replied, 'Sometimes in our lives, we are all lost young man. The trick though, is knowing that there is always a way back.' Then he casually released another page out the window and into the arms of the waiting wind.

Since the old man had still not looked at him, my friend asked with a curious voice, 'How do you know that I'm young?'

'I heard your footsteps running up the stairs as you were following Cassandra but when you came in the room you were not out of breath, which means not only are you young, but also in fairly good physical condition,' the old man replied as he set down his pen and turned around to view his visitor. 'And a soldier, as well, I see.'

'Cassandra?' the soldier asked confused by this new name the old man had just mentioned.

'Oh, excuse my manners. We so rarely get visitors here. My name is Erasmus and this falcon is Cassandra, a close friend and trusted advisor,' the old man answered motioning towards the bird, that now flew down from her perch atop a bookcase and landed on the desk next to the elderly gentleman, 'and one of my more dependable helpers.'

'My name is William, sir and if you don't mind my asking, what exactly do you do here?'

'We, my young friend,' he replied as he smiled and slipped in a wink towards Cassandra, 'are the keeper of all things lost and forgotten.'

'Lost and forgotten things?'

'Yes,' the old man reaffirmed, 'lost and forgotten things, until they are needed again.'

Seeing that the soldier was still puzzled, the old man continued his explanation, 'Here we collect the great works of art, stories, music, inventions, discoveries and ideas that humanity has created and then lost or forgotten. Here, we keep those treasures safe, until we feel the call from a man, woman or child whose pain could be eased or life made better by one of these forgotten treasures and then we arrange for these treasures to be discovered again.'

'Treasure like gold and jewels?'

'We do have some things here that contain those objects, like the Fabergé Egg in that corner. But jewels by themselves are only as valuable as a child's shiny trinkets. Gold, in too great of a quantity, can often just weigh you down. But do you know what is far better than this work of art?' the old man asked while picking up the Fabergé Egg. 'Stories! Stories, that inspire hope, creativity, empathy and compassion. Medicines that heal the sick, forgotten victories of the human mind that used rational thought, logic and reason to triumph over superstition and ignorance. I knew another man named William once, whose stories I constantly send out, who wrote "Our faults lie not in our stars but in ourselves." And music! Music, the universal language of God. Music, a language that never needs translation. It can soothe the afflicted, bring peace to the tormented and hasten the healing of wounds both physical and spiritual. And the best thing about all these treasures that I have just mentioned, is that they enrich the person that they are given to, without making the giver any poorer. But enough about me. As I've mentioned before, I see you have decided to become a soldier. What would you say is the most important quality for a soldier to have?'

'My army instructors said that in battle it is training but I believe that for a soldier the most important thing is … courage.'

'Courage? Courage.' the old man replied as he mulled over the word. 'Excellent answer, courage matters in any battles or fights you face in life, but what matters far more is what you are fighting for.'

"And so started his discussion with the wisest teacher, my friend, the Lieutenant, said that he had ever met. He told me that he learned more in those few hours, than he had in all his days, months and even years at school. They talked on a seemingly endless array of subjects. The old man had a way of taking many of life's most complicated questions and capturing the essence of the answers in sentences so simple that anyone could understand."

"Like what?" the child asked.

"Like, that in life words matter, but deeds matter far more and the results of those deeds matter the most. Before you follow men who tell you to destroy something, make them show you something that they have built that is better. It is far easier to destroy than to create. For example, it takes thousands of skilled, hard working individuals to build an ocean liner but any idiot with a stick of dynamite can sink it. All he has really proven is that he can accomplish something that any large chunk of ice floating in the water can do without even trying. Power, like money is important, but what is more important is how you get it and then what you do with it. Loyalty is important, but who or what you are loyal to is far more important. Trust, have faith, but check the facts because sometimes something that was true today will not be true tomorrow. And do not ignore inconvenient facts. Beware of any individual or ideology that claims to have all the answers but does not tolerate any questions. Beware anyone who espouses the belief that all your troubles and failures are the fault of others, though such an individual will never lack for followers."

"How did the old man know all these things?" the child inquired.

"My friend said it was because the old man studied history! History is the fascinating story of man repeating the same mistakes over and over again. The same mistake, so many times, that many people see only despair and sorrow in the future. But my friend said that Erasmus had a way of studying history that saw hope and infinite possibilities for the advancement and happiness of everyone."

"How?" the child insisted once again.

"By not only studying history but by carefully learning its lessons. Erasmus told him to study and honor the people that have moved humanity forward. Do not dwell on the monstrous injustices done by humanity to humanity, since the dawn of mankind, more than you study how these wrongs and injustices were corrected. The study of the individuals and civilizations that overcame these evils is the key to mankind moving forward. Also, judge individuals, nations and civilizations by the times in which they existed. It is easy to criticize the child labor of the industrial revolution, just as it will be easy for our descendants to criticize our destruction of the earth's forests, despite the warnings of places like Easter Island. People who lived in the past are responsible for the past. We are responsible for now and the future. The unique magic of being human is that, "if we listen to our better angel" we have the ability to leave the earth a better place than it was before we were born.

To achieve that, one must always be aware of evil. Evil comes in many disguises; nationalism, religion or ethnic and class differences. Quite often it has a brilliant mask and a voice that mixes a little truth to help distract from its myriad of lies, but in the end, evil's deeds always force it to reveal itself. Evil, can also be unbelievably patient, therefore, good and civilization must be ever vigilant. History has too often shown that civilizations are at their most vulnerable the longer they have peace and prosperity. Its citizens, that had inherited its bounty, then tend to forget the sacrifices and efforts their ancestors gave to get them there. What a thousand generations took to build can be lost by a single generation's carelessness, insouciance or simple indifference.

In 400 A.D., in the Western Roman Empire, you could travel thousands of miles, from Petra in Jordan, to Bath in Britain, on safe roads, through cities with lit streets, sanitation systems, and hot and cold running water. During your journey you could stop in the city of Rome itself, crossing rivers on bridges so well built that they are still in use to this day. Roman engineers, invented concrete, discovered the secrets of building archways and domed ceilings. They had already started to develop the steam engine, but by 475 A.D. it had all collapsed with the abdication of the Emperor Romulus and the breakup of Europe among the warring barbarian tribes. All the great libraries were destroyed, the aqueducts and coliseums fell into disrepair and humanity would have to go through centuries of darkness, where life would be, 'short, harsh and brutish.'

Humanity would not reach the standard of living that it enjoyed under Rome until over thirteen hundred years had passed. Among the many catalysts of this rebirth, was the rediscovery and development of the steam engine which brought about the beginning of the Industrial Revolution in the 1850s. But Rome, like all great civilizations, was not an area of land, a population of a certain peoples, tribe, ethnicity or religion. It was a set of ideals that were constantly being re-evaluated and improved upon.

The improvement of the health and happiness of all humans came step-by-step, using God's gifts of logic and reason, tempered by compassion. The descendants of the barbarians that destroyed Rome, marveled at its ruins for centuries, and strived to figure out a way to put back together, what they had in their ignorance destroyed. During the Dark and Medieval Ages, men used to look in wonderment upon the Roman ruins and ponder who were these people that could build these great cities. As late as the 1780s the British historian, Gibbon, was so awed by the ruins of Roman edifices and structures that no one could replicate as late as the 1800s, that he was inspired to write, 'The Decline and Fall of the Roman Empire.'

Erasmus told my friend that in truth there are only two types of humans; those of good will, who care about others and those who care only about themselves. The latter like to divide the world into us and them. But in the truly great battles of humanity, you fight for everyone or you fight for no-one.

Beware those who profit and thrive on chaos, anarchy and hatred. Beware of men who twist the truth or accuse the innocent scapegoat without proof, so they may more easily seduce the gullible, ignorant and desperate to follow them. Good, spreads its ideas by persuasion and reason, and if it makes a mistake, reason and logic cause it to change its path,

while evil will always cling desperately to its lies. Evil usually needs the sword to spread its ideas and often can be stopped by no other way. Jonas Salk did not have to threaten mothers to use his polio vaccine. No-one needed a gun to force people to use Thomas Edison's electric light, John Harrison's sea clock, Cai Lun's paper, Guttenberg's printing press or Louis Pasteur's pasteurization. Beware governments that use armies, police and walls to keep their own citizens contained and silent. And most importantly, like Thomas Edison, Andrew Carnegie or George Orwell, if you do make a mistake in your life, announce it as loudly as your triumphs, so that others do not have to make the same errors.

Erasmus and my friend could have easily talked all night but then a clock in the room chimed the hour, causing the Lieutenant to suddenly rise from his seat. 'My God,' he exclaimed in a near panic voice, 'how am I going to get back to my base?'

'Well, how did you get here?' Erasmus calmly inquired.

'I fell asleep in a small fishing boat that must have become un-moored and I awoke when it ran aground on the beach below.'

'Then I think the best plan would be to get back to that boat. Cassandra, will you please lead the way?'

As if she had been anticipating the request, the falcon quickly spread her wings and within seconds was out the door with Erasmus and the Lieutenant following closely behind. The unlikely trio made their way back through the myriad of halls and rooms of the castle and the Lieutenant marveled at the effortlessness of the elderly man's ability to keep up with Cassandra's swift flight. Moments later, as they were passing through the clock room, he could have sworn that the clocks ceased their ticking when Erasmus entered, and resumed as he exited, but decided that his mind was playing tricks on him. Before long, they were outside the castle walls, down the cliff steps and standing beside the vessel that was still aground on the beach with Cassandra perched atop the mast.

Gazing at the endless span of ocean before them, the Lieutenant exclaimed sarcastically, 'Great! This is just great! How on God's earth am I going to make tomorrow morning's roll call?'

'Stay calm Lieutenant. There is always a solution to everything. But if you don't mind, first I'd like to give you a little gift as a remembrance of our meeting.' The old man then handed him a small sealed wooden box about the size of a fist. 'I want you to open it when you are the most worried and scared that you think you will ever be.'

Momentarily distracted, he turned the box over in his hands and could hear something rattling inside of it. 'How will I know when that will be? Because right now sure seems like a contender.'

'Don't worry, you'll know.'

'Provided I get out of here, I'm heading directly into a combat zone. Do you think it should be before my first battle?'

'Don't worry, you'll know.'

'Well, sir, if I'm not back at my base by tomorrow morning this box will be opened in less than twelve hours.' He then slipped the small box into his jacket pocket and said, 'But I do thank you, it is very kind.' Once again the Lieutenant looked across the night ocean. He then sat down on the pile of sails and nets in back of the small boat and sighed in frustration. 'How am I going to get to tomorrow?'

'I have found that often the safest way to reach tomorrow is sleep,' Erasmus replied.

'I appreciate the words sir, but now is not the time for an esoteric discussion. I need a serious solution.'

'But I am offering you a serious solution young man. I mean no disrespect, but humor me for a moment. Lie back against the boat's side, close your eyes and tell me what you see.'

The Lieutenant relaxed against the side of the boat, closed his eyes and after several seconds said, 'I see nothing.'

'I know you think that you are answering truthfully but I do not quite believe your answer is correct, so if you will tolerate me a little longer, let us try once again from a different angle. What do you see with your ears?'

The Lieutenant smiled wryly and replied, 'I see nothing with my ears, sir.'

'Ahh, now that, I believe, so please, once more close your eyes and tell me what you see.'

The Safest Way Into Tomorrow
(Page 70)

The Lieutenant relaxed a little more into the folded sails and netting. As he was closing his eyes he thought he saw Erasmus step back, raise his cloaked arms outward and then pull them back as if beckoning the tide to come in. Ever so subtly, he felt the boat gently re-floating on the rising water and before he could open his eyes to answer Erasmus' question, he had fallen into a deep sleep, where dreams, like oceans, have their currents that will take you where they will.

Mozart and Memories
(Page 77)

The next morning, the Lieutenant felt himself being gently awakened by a fisherman asking him if he was alright. The Lieutenant, realizing how hungover and disheveled he must have looked, was extremely embarrassed. Forcing his mind out of its slumber, he apologized for having used the man's boat as a bed to sleep off the previous night's over-indulgences. The boat's owner reassured him that it was perfectly alright but since the Lieutenant still looked a little shaken, once again, asked if he needed any help.

'No, no, I'm fine,' the Lieutenant insisted. 'I had a little too much to drink last night, and had the strangest dreams you could ever imagine with castles, a strange old man and a falcon called Cassandra.'

The fisherman laughed, 'Must have been quite a night. What were you drinking?'

'I wish I could remember that as well as the dream. But speaking of remembering, you don't happen to know where the bus to the military base stops around here?'

'Couldn't be closer soldier; just follow the dock to the end where you'll see a small hotel. The bus stops right in front of it.'

The Lieutenant thanked the man for all his help and started down the dock while trying to smooth the wrinkles out of his uniform. As he neared the hotel he felt something in his jacket pocket. Reaching in, he came to a complete stop as he pulled out a small, sealed, wooden box. Five minutes earlier, he was certain that it all was a dream, but if it was a dream, where did he get the box and what was in it? He was just about to break it open, but then, recalling Erasmus's instructions, he returned it to his pocket and continued

on his way back to his unit. Three days later he was in the jungles of Cambodia.

By this point in the war, the Communist Khmer Rouge Army, under the command of Pol Pot had already taken control of huge areas of the country. They enforced their rule by the use of unlimited fear and terror. Buildings and books, both new and ancient were wantonly destroyed. Not only were captured Cambodian soldiers executed but also countless innocent civilians. Men, women and children were lined up in fields and slaughtered by being clubbed to death with a metal bar. This method was used because Pol Pot and his minions did not believe in wasting a bullet on them. Fathers were executed in front of their families, mothers in front of their children and children of any age in front of their parents' corpses. Sometimes, the condemned were forced to dig their own graves but more often than not, they were just left on the ground, creating acres and acres of dead bodies that would later become known as the 'Killing Fields.' When once asked to give mercy to a mother and her children, Pol Pot replied 'To keep you alive is no benefit and to destroy you is no loss.'

Within his very first day on patrol, the Lieutenant and his platoon attacked a squad of Khmer Rouge soldiers who were executing a group of farmers. Having the element of surprise, they quickly won the small skirmish and ended up with two enemy prisoners whom he interrogated before having them helicoptered to a prison camp. From these prisoners he learned that according to the Khmer Rouge's policy, it seemed that anything justified the murdering of civilians. If they were followers of any religion, kill them. If they were educated, kill them. If they were Thai, teachers, doctors, wore glasses or jewelry, kill them. Even if they believed in a form of communism different than their own, kill them. And kill, did not only mean the individuals involved alone, but their family, friends and sometimes even their entire town or village as well. But the thing that shocked him the most about his prisoners, was not only were they not ashamed of what they had done, but that they had been photographing every killing, including infants, as if they were truly convinced that what they were doing was so noble that it needed to be recorded for posterity. It was as if an entire population had been led by a handful of madmen, into a collective insanity, so surreal, that it would cause any outsider to doubt their own senses. Doubt whether they were awake or asleep within the clutches of a horrible nightmare. But they were awake and the monsters within this nightmare had only just begun their conjuring.

For the rest of his tour of duty, the Lieutenant would witness an evil so confident, it needed no mask. This was not war, this was genocide. The civilians he found dead were not killed by the collateral damage of a battle but by deliberate calculated murder.

Month after month went by as he and his troops were helicoptered to the areas where they were most needed. The fact that he and his men were making a difference, kept him going. That and the talks he would have with his wife by radio every time they were back at base. He and his men knew they were not saving the world, but each life they did save, counted. Every murderer he stopped not only saved a life but made other murderers sleep a little less easy. They made other murderers know that there were men out there, who would not look away, and even more importantly, would confront them.

The Lieutenant was two weeks short of completing his year on the front lines when he was ordered to take a platoon deep into the jungle near the Thai border, where there were reports of an enemy build up. The Lieutenant was a little more nervous on this patrol because several of his men were new recruits and he would have to keep a keen eye on them as they learned the ropes. He would have to teach them in the field how to move silently; to recognize the signs of buried landmines, trip wires and most of all that silence in the jungle is usually a foreshadowing of an impending ambush.

Intelligence had informed them that a new enemy build up had just begun and they would be dropped off by several Huey helicopters right after nightfall. The insertion went off perfectly, but within minutes of the last Huey departing, his platoon started taking fire from all sides. Realizing that they had been dropped right in the middle of an entire enemy regiment, he radioed his situation back to base and then started moving his division towards a pre-designated landing zone where, the Hueys would extract his platoon.

With his staff sergeant leading the way, the Lieutenant, who usually took point, instead took the rear guard position. With mortar shells and RPGs exploding all around them, he had to keep the new recruits from freezing and becoming an easy target. Machine gun tracers glowed eerily as they clipped pieces of foliage or lodged in tree trunks with a thud. 'Fire and move!' the Lieutenant screamed, as he yanked a frightened private who was just about to dive into a sheltering ditch. When the private still hesitated, he kicked aside some leaves at the bottom of the ditch, revealing sharpened punji sticks. 'It's a trick as old as Julius Caeser, now move!' Seeing the death he had just avoided, snapped the soldier back to reality and he started running rapidly towards the clearing where the first Huey was just touching down. One by one they piled in as the Lieutenant covered their withdrawal. As he scanned the jungle, a figure appeared in his sights, but since the figure was bending over a wounded enemy soldier, he delayed pulling the trigger, thinking that he might be a medic. In that moment of hesitation, a mortar round exploded, riddling his body with shrapnel as it threw him to the ground. Raising his head he saw that all his men were already safely airborne except for the few on the last helicopter which was waiting for him. Seeing that he was hit, his sergeant was about to get out to try to get him aboard. The Lieutenant, knowing how badly he was wounded, knew that there was no way that his sergeant could get him on board before the enemy would take out the Huey. Making eye contact with the pilot, he signaled him to take off. The pilot gunned the engines taking the helicopter and his men safely into the sheltering arms of the night sky.

Another Way You Can Die
(Page 88)

Weak from loss of blood, he saw a gathering of shadows cautiously approaching him. When they realized that he was too shot up to be a threat, the enemy gathered around him and started to search his pockets and knapsack. Suddenly, the Khmer Rouge soldiers, all stood up and looked to the east, where they could see two Huey helicopters approaching, followed by the distinctive silhouette of an AC-130 Spectre Gunship giving suppression fire with every weapon it possessed. The Lieutenant's men had not given up on him.

Realizing the massive firepower that would soon be raking the jungle as the Hueys and AC-130 Spectre Gunship tried to rescue the American officer, the enemy soldiers grabbed each of the Lieutenant's limbs and started running for the safety of the jungle canopy where their camp was hidden. Every second they were running with the Lieutenant's bleeding body brought him unimaginable pain and every second seemed to last an eternity. There seemed to be an infinite number of those seconds. Rockets and artillery shells exploded both far and near, until finally, the Khmer Rouge soldiers arrived at a barbed wire compound. Finally, feeling safe, they dragged his body into a solitary bamboo hut and dropped him on the floor. The last thing he remembered was the fading sound of helicopters as they gave up the search and returned to base.

Toccata-Carpimus Noctem
(Page 96)

Night Castle — Part II

The Lion's Roar

(Page 102)

The Lieutenant remained a prisoner at the Khmer Rouge camp for over two months. From the first day he was constantly interrogated for military information but would never tell them anything beyond his name, rank and serial number. During that time, he never received any medical care for his numerous wounds that were steadily getting worse. He believed that the only reason he was not executed was the Khmer's hope that he might reveal something useful before he died. With the infections that were spreading unchecked around the shrapnel still in his body, he was also aware that his death, was at best, only days away.

During his time in captivity, he learned to cherish the night, for since the camp had no electricity, his captors tended to leave him alone in his cell. It was also at night, that a cool breeze from a nearby stream somehow made its way through his small window and removed the stifling heat that tormented him throughout the day. Night, became his friend and was fairly dependable at keeping his captors away, but on this night, things would be different. Without any warning, his cell door unexpectedly swung open. A man wearing the uniform of a communist officer entered catching the Lieutenant off guard while writing in a loose-leaf book he had salvaged from a junk pile. For a pen, he was using a sharpened stick that he would dip in a small jar that contained a mixture of charcoal and his own blood, forming a fairly decent ink. Of course, all of this was forbidden and was cause enough for instant execution.

The Lieutenant recognized the man as General Tran-Do. He had been briefed about him numerous times since his arrival in Indochina. Tran-Do had been involved in the Indochina war for many years and had a reputation as a formidable front-line officer. The Lieutenant had seen him at various times giving orders throughout the camp but never had any direct contact with him.

Towering over the prisoner sitting on the floor, the Communist General demanded to know what he was doing. The Lieutenant, who at this point was aware that he was close to death and that answering the General's question would give away no military secrets, risked nothing by telling the truth. 'I just finished a story I was writing.'

'What type of story?' the General snapped back.

'It's a fairytale called, "The Dreams of Fireflies."'

Slightly taken aback by the answer from a prisoner that his best interrogators could get nothing out of beyond his name and rank, the General reached down and snatched the pages from his hand. A quick glance confirmed that it was indeed a fairytale. 'And why would you be doing such a thing, prisoner?'

'About a year ago, when I was back at base, I called my wife and she had told me that she was pregnant. The child was born a little less than half a year ago and I now know that I will never live to see my child. This may seem odd to you, but most American men dream of having a kid to throw a baseball with, take to their first New York Yankees game. A child to hold and just watch grow up as we get to know each other. Since the day of my capture, I realized that my child and I would never meet, but I found a bunch of old notebooks in a trash pile and I took them. I always imagined myself making up fairytales that I would tell my child at night, but since I now know that is not to be, I came up with a crazy plan. I decided that I would write fifty short fairytales, and as each one was finished, I would place my wife's name and address at the end, roll it up, put it into one of the countless Coca-Cola bottles in the trash pile, seal it with tree bark and then drop it into the stream which I know runs into a river, that runs into the ocean. Perhaps, I thought, with a little luck, a few of those bottles might make it to my family. I may never get to teach my kid how to play baseball, but if even one of these letters gets back, my child might feel like we've met and got to know each other in our own way. I've already completed and slipped forty-nine into the stream. The one in your hand is number fifty. The last and final one.'

Tran-Do stared intently at his prisoner. 'Your story does not make any sense. I know a great deal about American military codes. If your wife was pregnant you could have asked for compassionate leave. They would have allowed you to return home to see your wife and child.'

'That is true. My wife and I did discuss it, but we decided that she was safe, as would be our child. While here, defenseless women and children are being murdered so casually that someone needed to help save them. If not me, who? If in America, an insane group of individuals took control of the country, killed me and were going to murder my family, I would hope that someone from another area of the world that had not slipped into the clutches of insanity and evil, would come and protect them. So together, my wife and I decided that I would try to finish what I had come here to do.'

'You did not need to come here to protect anyone. Protection of all Southeast Asians is our intent, our purpose.' Tran-Do shot back.

'A friend of mine, Erasmus, once told me that there is the morality of intentions and the morality of results. The fields all around us are filled with dead women and children with their skulls caved in by iron axle rods. Your intentions sir, differ from your results.'

'They could have been killed by your American bombs.'

'Bombs, sir, do not tie women's and children's hands behind their backs before killing them.'

'Who is this man, Erasmus? A U.S. officer?'

The Lieutenant laughed and then recounted all he could remember from his encounter on that faraway night. He even included the part about the box Erasmus told him not to open until he was the most afraid he thought he would ever be.

Tran-Do, then inquired if he had opened it during his first battle. The Lieutenant smiled and shook his head no, and replied, 'I opened it back in Phnom-Penh when I was waiting to hear if my child was born safe and healthy.'

'What did this box contain?'

'Believe it or not, just a simple wind up music box that played a piece by Bach. But it did help keep me calm until I received the good news; ten toes, ten fingers, and healthy. I went right out to the PX and bought a leather Spalding baseball to stay in practice.'

The General smiled and mentioned how several of his officers had argued for hours about that baseball and its possible significance when they found it among the Lieutenants possessions. Tran-Do then asked why he had gotten married and had a child if he knew that he was going to volunteer for such a dangerous assignment. The Lieutenant said that he had felt unusually blessed to have been born into the safety of the world of Western Civilization, but many are not. So, he decided that he would devote twenty years of his life to joining the military and try his best to make the world a better place. After that, he thought he would retire from the army, meet some nice girl, get married and raise a wagonload of kids. But true love cares naught about the plans of humans and will appear when it decides.

'Where did you meet your wife?' Tran-Do queried.

The Lieutenant then told him how they had met and fallen in love in his last days in New York City right before his deployment overseas.

Dreams We Conceive
(Page 108)

He explained that even though they only had one night alone together as newlyweds, it seems one night is sometimes all you need. As you know, it was barely two months later that he got the call telling him that he was going to be a father. At this point, Tran-Do could see that the telling of his story had exhausted the man and the Lieutenant slowly slid down the wall to the floor, where he passed out from exhaustion. Tran-Do, looked down at his unconscious prisoner and then at the pieces of paper containing the American soldier's final fairytale. Walking out of the cell, he bolted the door and walked towards the cooking fire burning near the center of the camp intending to cast the pages in, but for a reason he himself could not explain, he walked past the fire, to the edge of the compound, where he picked up an empty Coke bottle. He then walked up to the little stream that snaked down to the river below, carefully rolled up the final story, slipped it into the bottle and used a piece of a small stick as a cork. Tran-Do then gently placed the bottle into the stream.

The General then stood and watched as it slowly started its journey towards the sea, the green glass glistening in the moonlight. As he watched it drift away, his mind wandered. The American reminded him of himself and that thought alone made him strangely uncomfortable. The Lieutenant seemed well educated, idealistic and had joined the military for similar reasons as he had. To make the world a better place.

Tran-Do had joined this army to make Southeast Asia a paradise for all Southeast Asians, but had instead personally overseen the killing of thousands of innocent people and his organization as a whole had killed millions. How had he, who as a child had been so carefully, taught the Confucian ideals of compassion by his mother, become part of this? The Lieutenant, who was dying did not seem to fear death, except in how it would affect his wife and newborn. While Tran-Do, who was not in any imminent danger, not only feared death, but now feared life and what each new day would require of him. How could he, who had always envisioned himself as being so enlightened, convinced that he was saving the Southeast Asian people, instead, somehow become their executioner? Meanwhile, this imperialist soldier, that he had despised, had left the safety of his world, to come to the jungles of Cambodia, to save and bring the most important freedom, the freedom from fear and death, to people that he did not even know.

In their earlier discussion the Lieutenant had told him how Erasmus said, 'In life, you fight for the good of everyone or in truth you are fighting for no one.' Erasmus also believed that in the end, 'God would save everyone, even Satan.' Tran-Do, being a communist, was an avowed atheist but he found Erasmus's point of view most interesting.

Now, even though the General was in good health, he had gone many days without sleep, and lack of sleep can blur the line between reality and dreams, the present and the past. So it did not alarm Tran-Do when in the evening mist on the banks of the stream, he saw the ghostly apparitions of his mother and himself as a young boy being taught the ethics of Confucius.

Mother and Son

(Mother)

REMEMBER WHAT CONFUCIUS TAUGHT, ALWAYS BE KIND.

(Son)

YES, MOTHER.

(Mother)

ALWAYS HELP THE WEAK AND THE OLD.

(Son)

YES, MOTHER. I UNDERSTAND.

(Mother)

AND ALWAYS HELP THOSE LESS FORTUNATE THAN YOURSELF.

(Son)

YES, MOTHER. ALWAYS.

A jet passes by in the distance and the apparition of his mother fades away. The child turns towards Tran-Do in a non-judgmental but puzzled voice.

(Son)

HOW DID I BECOME YOU?

The General looked back towards the apparition of himself as a child who neither spoke nor disappeared, but only waited for his answer. Forced to examine the actions of his entire life, he tried to figure out at what point he had become the person who would murder an unarmed man whom was only suspected of not supporting their cause. At what point did he become a man able to look away when others gave the order to murder a suspect's family, then murder the entire village? Is not stopping a murder, when you have the ability to do so, the same as committing the murder yourself?

Initially, as a young man, he had believed the men who told him they would have to do these inhumane acts, but once they had completed these evil deeds, they would have created a utopia for all people, for all time. A utopia, where all would be equal and the world at peace. He now knew it was a lie. The only equality he was bringing the masses, was the equality of death. The only peace they were bringing, was the eternal peace of the grave. The entire cause this war was being fought for was a lie. He now knew that, just as the men who had recruited him into "the cause" must have known. But he had so much invested in the lie, that he never allowed himself to admit that it was a lie, and still worse, he perpetuated the lies to others.

All this time, he was wrestling with a way to answer the question from this apparition of himself as a child. This child, who still silently awaited his answer, refused to disappear. So, he started to put his thoughts into words, and as he spoke he began to see a possible way out of this night.

There Was a Life
(Page 117)

True, he could not bring back to life the innocent lives that had been taken, but he could quit this army of evil, do no more evil in this army's name and most importantly, he could save the life of this young lieutenant and get him back safely to his family. It was still dark; he could easily go to the supply hut, take a knapsack of food and medicine, release the American officer from his cell and get him to the Thai border, where he would be safe. He was aware that at dawn, when they realized not only had the prisoner escaped but the General had deserted as well, they would throw as many troops as possible into their pursuit. But he had a plan even for that possibility. If that eventuality occurred, he would send the Lieutenant down a secret path to Thailand where the Thai border guards would immediately take care of him. Then he would leave an obvious trail to throw the Khmer Rouge off the Lieutenant's track, even though he knew that his capture would probably lead to his own death.

He found it strange that the chance of losing his own life now worried him far less than the possibility that if they were ever to meet again in the future, would the Lieutenant embrace him as a friend, or turn away from him as a participant in genocide. A murderer, not only of lives, but of compassion and tolerance. Still, either way, it did not matter, the die was cast, the Rubicon about to be crossed and the Lieutenant saved.

Tran-Do walked across the camp and looked through the slats on the Lieutenant's cell door where the Lieutenant was still peacefully sleeping. In the far distance he could hear the falling of B-52 bombs on an area where he knew the Khmer Rouge had an ammo dump. Anti-aircraft fire was filling the sky and a sudden huge secondary explosion let him know that one of the bombs had found its target. The explosions distracted the guards with its impromptu fireworks display which the General used as a perfect opportunity to enter the supply hut unobserved. But those same distant explosions also caused the Lieutenant's dreams to become more fitful.

Moonlight and Madness
(Page 134)

Meanwhile, as Tran-Do was preparing for the Lieutenant's and his escape, the B-52s faded away and the Lieutenant awoke. Pulling himself up the bamboo wall, the American looked out the window at the moon, realizing that somewhere on this night, his wife and child would be looking at that same moon. He had no regrets about the results of his decision but he regretted how it might affect his child's life, the child he was still convinced he would never see.

Time Floats On
(Page 144)

He looked and wondered but could only hold himself up for a short while before he once again slipped to the ground and fell asleep. During that time, Tran-Do had finished collecting the necessary supplies and with perfect timing, slipped across the compound and unbolted the cell's door. The Lieutenant was still curled up on the floor, in a fetal position. Setting down the knapsack of supplies Tran-Do softly whispered, 'Lieutenant, wake up,' then in a slightly louder voice, 'Lieutenant, wake up! I'm getting you out of here!'

When he still did not stir and knowing that speed was essential, the General gently started to lift him up but the Lieutenant's body was cold and limp. Tran-Do froze as he realized that the man in his arms had just died. Died so recently that rigor mortis had not even set in. Stunned in disbelief, he gently lowered the body back to the earth and leaving the knapsack of supplies behind, exited the cell.

He walked to the very furthest part of the camp and stood on the edge of the cliff that overlooked a deep valley that the river had carved into the soft rock over thousands of years. On the rocks below, there were the bones of prisoners who had thrown themselves off to escape their Khmer Rouge tormentors. He had never thought about them before, but now he did and he found himself contemplating doing the same. His one hope for salvation, the saving of this one good man was gone. This man that he had known less than a day. This man whom he felt closer to than men he had known his entire life. If he was incapable of doing any good in this world, why not just end his life? This way at the very least he could do no more evil.

As he stood at the edge of the cliff, the weight of the evil deeds from his past urged him to throw himself into the abyss and end it all. But every time he was about to take that final step into the void, something stopped him. What that something was, he could not figure out, as he went over and over it in his mind. Who was Tran-Do? The real Tran-Do? Was he the innocent child who once wanted to become a Confucius monk? Was he the idealistic youth who really believed he could change the world with every neuron in his mind? The youth who readily embraced idealism while ignoring the reality of human flaws? Was it the officer who oversaw not only the murder of innocent humans, but the

murder of humanity's saving graces of mercy, compassion and forgiveness? Was it the man who was willing to risk his own life to save the Lieutenant or did that even count, since the intention was never achieved?

Epiphany
(Page 149)

Then he recalled how the Greek philosopher, Salon, once said, 'You can never judge a life 'til it is over,' and though Tran-Do was only one step away from death, as of this moment, he was still quite alive. If he could not return the Lieutenant to his family alive, he could still leave this army of evil and with some luck, perhaps make it to America and let the Lieutenant's wife and child know that though he was dead, he had died saving others. He was a hero, who had died bringing hope to the hopeless and letting those who thought the world had forgotten them know that they were not forgotten.

It was still dark as he slipped back into the prison cell to get the knapsack of supplies. Before he left, he arranged the Lieutenant's body and noticed that a small area of the ground underneath where he had been sleeping looked slightly different. The earth in one corner was looser, as if something had been buried there. Digging into the ground, he discovered a small wooden box containing a hand-wound music box.

Bach Lullaby

(Page 168)

Placing the box in his knapsack, he finished laying out the body and then left, bolting the door behind him. Calling out for the Khmer Rouge captain of the guard, he berated him for allowing the American officer to die before getting more information out of him. He then showed him the wooden box he had discovered in the cell demanding to know how such a large piece of contraband could have gone undiscovered. As the guard started to stutter an answer, the General cut him off asking, 'How do you know that he did not also have a small handheld radio? How do you know that he has not radioed our location?' Once again before the guard could answer, Tran-Do cut him off and sternly ordered, 'Captain, we cannot afford to take any chances. Tomorrow, we move camp further up river but tonight you carefully bury that officer outside this compound. I do not want his body accidentally discovered by the Cambodian Army. And Captain, it is only because of your long service that you are not being buried with him.'

Knowing that fear of punishment would cause his commands to be unquestionably obeyed, the General, then turned and walked back into the camp headquarters' hut. There he retrieved the Lieutenant's dog tags, wallet and a well-worn baseball. Then he slipped out of the camp determined to somehow get to America, find the Lieutenant's wife and ask her forgiveness. He did not know how he would get there and, once there, how he would find her. But he was determined to do it.

He slipped out of the camp, following the river towards the coastline. The river constantly morphed its appearance on its way to the sea. Sometimes it was wide and meandering and at other times it narrowed into fast flowing rapids. But it was while following this river on his journey that he received his first piece of good fortune. Tran-Do reached a spot where the river turned wide and more importantly extremely shallow. There, stranded in the sandy river bottom of those shallows were the fifty Coca-Cola bottles containing the Lieutenant's fairytales to his child and at the bottom of each story was the Lieutenant's wife's address in New Jersey, U.S.A. Running about like an excited child, he collected all fifty bottles, removed all the pages and wrapped them in a watertight, canvas poncho before resuming his quest.

It took him many years, but eventually he arrived in America, only to be disappointed when the people who were living at the address he found in the bottles, said that the family had moved out quite a while ago and they had no idea where they were. In desperation, he went to Times Square in New York City to search for the drug dealer that the Lieutenant had told him about. He was lucky enough to find that the dealer still resided at the address the Lieutenant had placed in his wallet. The dealer immediately remembered the young officer and offered his assistance in finding out where the Lieutenant's family might have moved. The dealer enlisted the aid of a sympathetic policeman who helped him discover the wife's new location. Tran-Do now felt he had a real chance of completing his quest by asking the Lieutenant's wife's forgiveness for the death of her husband, a soldier who had gone to a far away land to protect the lives of others.

At this point in the story, the little girl looked at the stranger's black t-shirt with the initials for New York City printed boldly on the front. Slowly standing up, she said in soft but nervous voice, "Sir, you are the drug dealer."

"Why would you think such a thing?" he replied while also rising.

"Because, only he would know so much of the story."

"No, my child, I wish that I could say that I was that dealer, but I am Tran-Do. And you my dear, are the Lieutenant's child."

"But that's impossible," she answered in a shocked and confused voice. "The man's child was a boy. You said that he could not wait to teach him how to play baseball."

The man then reached into his satchel and took out something which he gently tossed to the little girl. She instinctively caught it and saw it was a worn leather baseball. "That is what your father wanted to do with you." He then reached once more into his satchel and took out a stack of pages neatly encased in a manila folder along with a small music box and handed it to the child. "These are the fairytales he wrote for you and the music box that holds the melody he listened to the night you were born."

"No! No, you've made a mistake. You have the wrong child," she insisted. "My mom told me that my father is in heaven but his name is Bill. Bill Cozier."

"Bill, little one, is short for William. He was Lieutenant William Cozier. I've been down here outside your home for nearly a week trying to gather the courage to ask for your mother's and your forgiveness but was unable to do so. This night, I built a fire and by its light a sandcastle modeled on the one your father described to me from when he met Erasmus. Then, by some miracle, you appeared. Child, many brave and great men over the centuries have fought for the safety and freedom of themselves, their families or their fellow citizens. But, men who risk all to save strangers, people that they have never met, to save men that would have killed them in a second if they had the chance… where do such individuals come from? God knows I don't think many of us deserve them. But they do exist and one of them was your father. To give up all to save your brother is a noble thing to do but to give up all to save your enemy… well that is something I cannot explain. Child, can you forgive me for your father's death? Could you… not hate me?"

A tear started to well up in the child's eye as she tried to take in all she had just learned. As the tear fell, it landed in the moat surrounding the sand castle just as a wave from the incoming tide reached the outer ends of the moat, pouring water in before temporarily retreating back to the ocean. The little girl looked at Tran-Do's eyes and she could see the pain of regret for an act that cannot be undone. "I don't hate you sir. I forgive you, and I think my mother will too. Come back with me and you can ask her yourself."

"I don't think I have that kind of courage. I would like to ask, if as a final kindness, you could ask her for me."

"But you do have the courage! You asked me."

"It's hard to explain, but sometimes it is easier to ask forgiveness from a child than a grown-up. And besides I have to be leaving now."

"Where do you have to go?"

"Somewhere there is a castle out there that I have to find." And after a gentle bow, Tran-Do turned and started walking away along the beach. As the child watched him fade away into the darkness, she suddenly realized that she was outside the house in the middle of the night and her mother was going to be incredibly angry when she discovered that she had snuck down to the beach.

Clutching the box, the baseball and her father's papers she started running up the sand dune stairs. She was running so hard, that she nearly fell when she collided with a beautiful young lady in a white gauze summer dress, on one of the landings. Helping the child to steady herself, the lady asked, "Where, my little one, are you running to in such a hurry?"

"I'm sorry I bumped into you, miss. I have to get back home! I shouldn't be out this late. I'm in big trouble!" the girl answered as she continued scrambling up the stairs towards the house.

"Don't worry," the lady answered, "you won't be in any trouble at all."

"You don't know my mom!" the girl shouted over her shoulder. Moments later she walked into her living room where her mother was watching television. When she saw her daughter coming in from the outside in her nightgown, her feet all covered with sand, holding a bevy of objects, her mother leapt to her feet and demanded to know where she had been. The child then explained all that had transpired that night and at the end handed her the folder of handwritten fairytales. The mother looked at the pages immediately recognizing her late husband's handwriting. Dropping the papers to the floor, she told her daughter to stay inside before running down to the beach to find this man that her daughter had told her about.

When she reached the area around the bonfire and sandcastle she could see footprints in the sand heading out into the darkness. Just as she was about to follow his trail, another wave from the incoming tide swept the footprints away. Realizing that to search for him aimlessly in the dark was useless, she looked back at the sandcastle being steadily eroded by the incoming waves. But the back tower still stood with a small chain hung around it. She picked it up, and by the bonfire's light, saw that it held her husband's dog tags.

The man was who he said he was. She had known that her husband had died in combat, but had always hoped that it was quick and painless. Now that she knew the entire story, she found herself talking to her late husband. There was a tenderness in her voice that would cause anyone who heard her, to know she was certain that the Lieutenant could hear every word.

Father, Son & Holy Ghost
(Page 169)

Finally exhausted from the cathartic outburst, she looked behind her and saw that her daughter had followed her and had witnessed her breakdown on the beach. Running over, she reached down, picked the girl up and carried her back to the house. There she held her in her arms and promised that everything would be alright, with the kind of reassurance that only a parent can give a child. She sang her a simple lullaby and then together they both drifted into a deep peaceful dream-filled slumber.

Remnants of a Lullaby
(Page 181)

Now, nights and dreams are quite common, but on this night, Morpheus himself, guided both mother and child through the labyrinths of Nod, to the exact same dream, where waiting for them both, was one, young Lieutenant Cozier.

The Safest Way Into Tomorrow (Reprise)
(Page 187)

Outside, the bonfire, though dying down, was still sending small armadas of sparks into the night breezes and in the sky, a lone falcon was silhouetted against the moon.

Embers
(Page 189)

After the End

It was twenty years later and Lieutenant Cozier's daughter was now a young lady, married, with three little girls of her own. It was early in the summer and the littlest child came running up holding a bottle that had just washed up on the shore. She handed it to her mother all excited because she could see that it contained a note. Lieutenant Cozier's daughter managed to dislodge the cork and pull out a single page letter. It said, "I have found my castle! Love, Tran-Do."

Child of the Night
(Page 195)

Believe
(Page 203)

Nutrocker
(Page 213)

Carmina Burana
(Page 224)

Tracers
(Page 231)

NIGHT ENCHANTED

Lyrics by
PAUL O'NEIL

Music by
GIUSEPPE VERDI, LEO DELIBES
and PAUL O'NEILL

Night Enchanted - 11 - 1

© 2009 WARNER-TAMERLANE PUBLISHING CORP. and PAUL O'NEILL PUBLISHING
All Rights Administered by WARNER-TAMERLANE PUBLISHING CORP.
All Rights Reserved

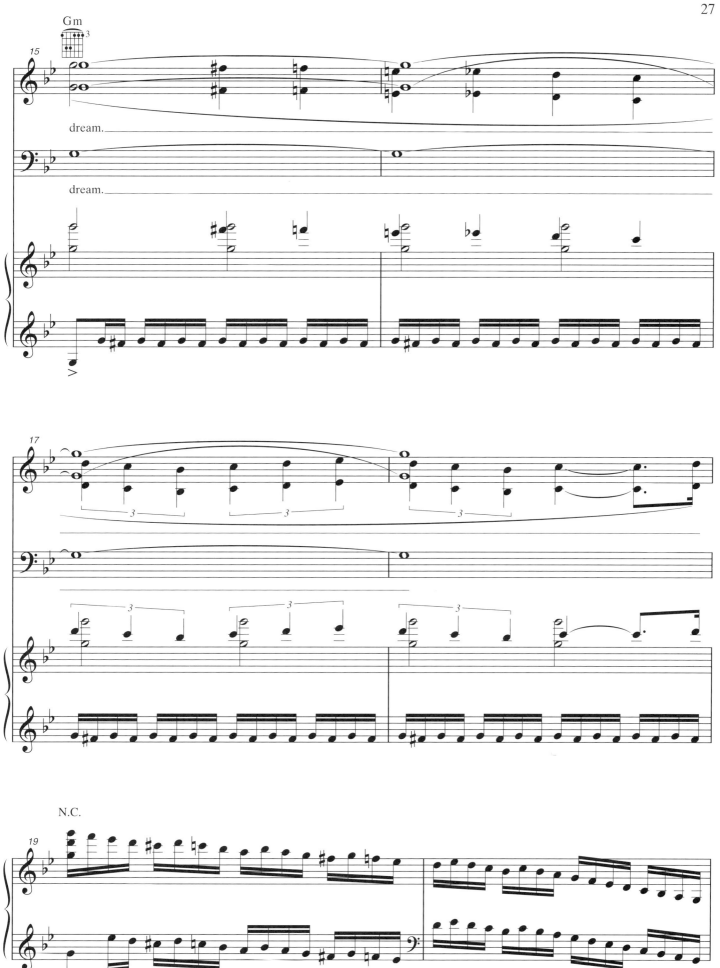

30

Ab | Db/F Ab/Gb | G Cm/Eb Db/F Ab/Gb | G Cm/Eb Db/F Ab/Gb | G Cm/Eb Db/F Ab/Gb

ty.   Hear us!   Hear us!   Hear us!

ty. For - ev - er,   for - ev - er,   for - ev - er,   for - ev - er,

G Bb Ab/C Eb | Gb F/A Cm D7 | G   N.C.

where our hopes have nev - er ceased to be.

G7(b9) | Cm/G G7 G7(b9) | Cm/G

Death   will em - brace   us,

Death   will em - brace   us,

32

Night Enchanted - 11 - 8

SPARKS

Sparks - 12 - 11

THE MOUNTAIN

**Based upon *Mars, the Bringer of War* from *The Planets* by GUSTAV HOLST
and *In The Hall of the Mountain King* by EDVARD GRIEG**

Arrangement and Additional Music by
PAUL O'NEILL and JOHN OLIVA

58

The Mountain - 10 - 6

NIGHT CASTLE

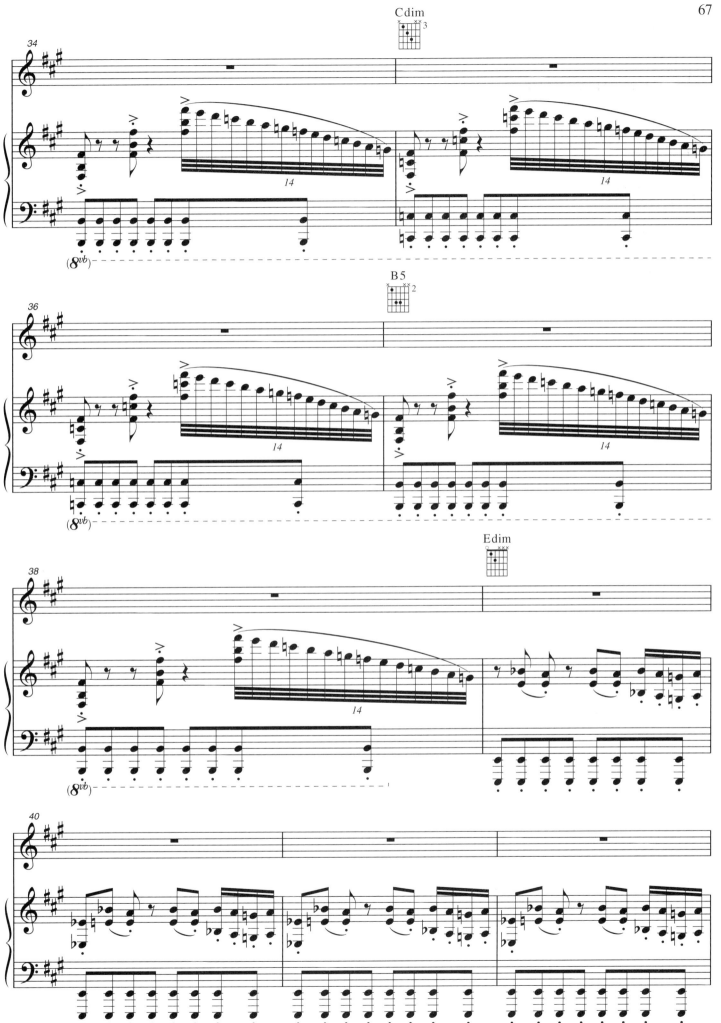

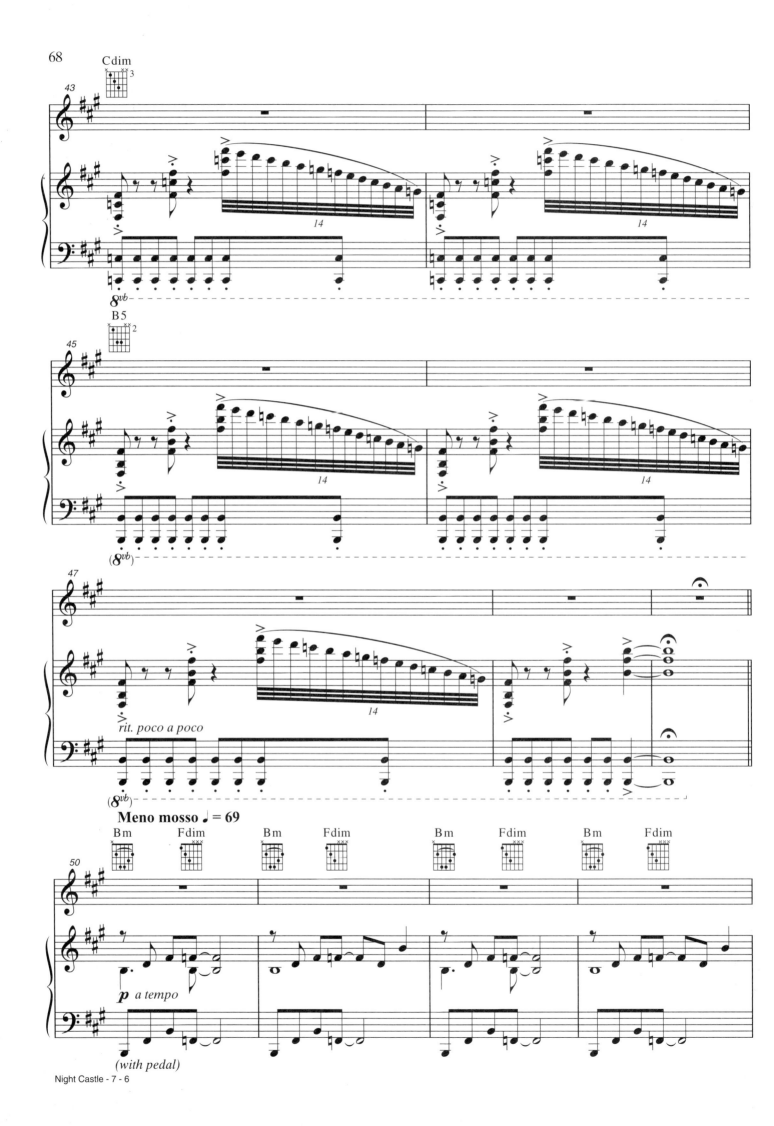

THE SAFEST WAY INTO TOMORROW

Lyrics by
PAUL O'NEILL

Music by
PAUL O'NEILL and JOHN OLIVA

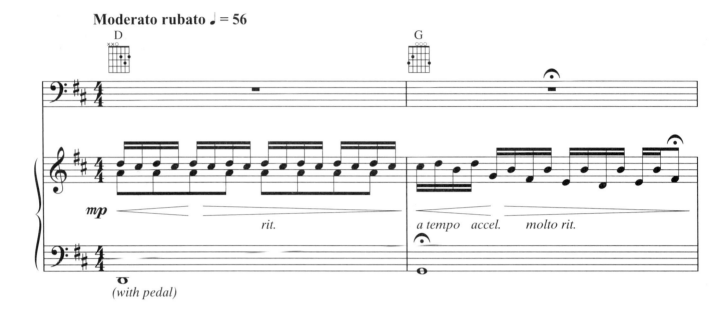

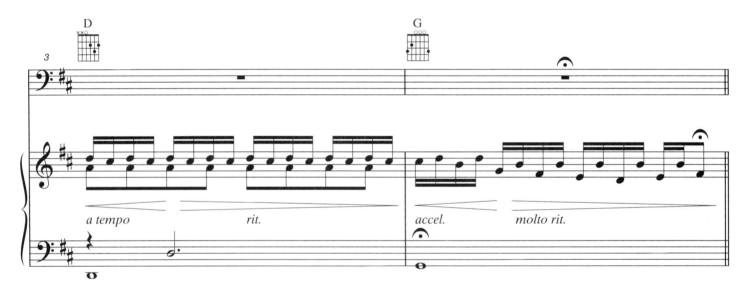

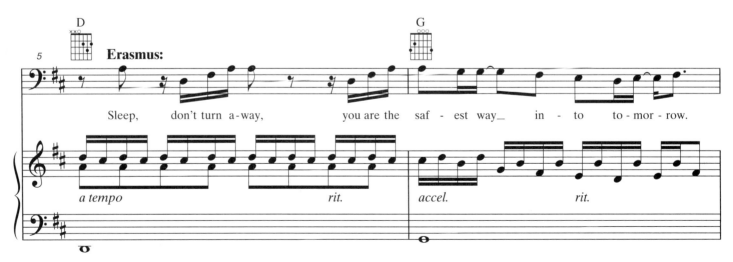

The Safest Way Into Tomorrow - 7 - 1

© 2009 WARNER-TAMERLANE PUBLISHING CORP., PAUL O'NEILL PUBLISHING, WB MUSIC CORP. and JOHN OLIVA PUBLISHING DESIGNEE
All Rights on behalf of itself and PAUL O'NEILL PUBLISHING Administered by WARNER-TAMERLANE PUBLISHING CORP.
All Rights on behalf of itself and JOHN OLIVA PUBLISHING DESIGNEE Administered by WB MUSIC CORP.
All Rights Reserved

The Safest Way Into Tomorrow - 7 - 6

MOZART AND MEMORIES
Based upon *Symphony No. 25* by WOLFGANG AMADEUS MOZART

Arrangement and Additional Music by
PAUL O'NEILL and JOHN OLIVA

Mozart and Memories - 11 - 1

© 2009 WARNER-TAMERLANE PUBLISHING CORP., PAUL O'NEILL PUBLISHING, WB MUSIC CORP. and JOHN OLIVA PUBLISHING DESIGNEE
All Rights on behalf of itself and PAUL O'NEILL PUBLISHING Administered by WARNER-TAMERLANE PUBLISHING CORP.
All Rights on behalf of itself and JOHN OLIVA PUBLISHING DESIGNEE Administered by WB MUSIC CORP.
All Rights Reserved

Mozart and Memories - 11 - 10

ANOTHER WAY YOU CAN DIE

Lyrics by
PAUL O'NEILL

Music by
PAUL O'NEILL and JOHN OLIVA

Another Way You Can Die - 8 - 1

© 2009 WARNER-TAMERLANE PUBLISHING CORP., PAUL O'NEILL PUBLISHING, WB MUSIC CORP. and JOHN OLIVA PUBLISHING DESIGNEE
All Rights on behalf of itself and PAUL O'NEILL PUBLISHING Administered by WARNER-TAMERLANE PUBLISHING CORP.
All Rights on behalf of itself and JOHN OLIVA PUBLISHING DESIGNEE Administered by WB MUSIC CORP.
All Rights Reserved

TOCCATA-CARPIMUS NOCTEM

Music by
J.S. BACH and PAUL O'NEILL

THE LION'S ROAR

Lyrics by
PAUL O'NEILL

Music by
PAUL O'NEILL and AL PITRELLI

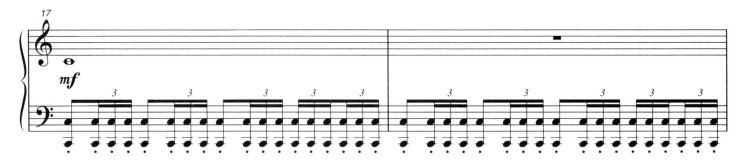
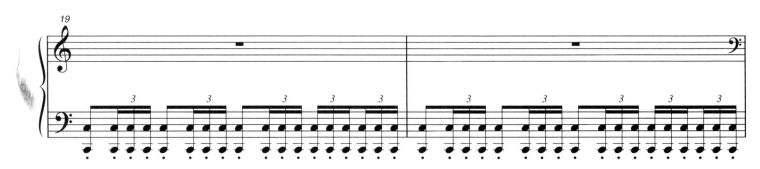

© 2009 WARNER-TAMERLANE PUBLISHING CORP., PAUL O'NEILL PUBLISHING and MIGHTY MUSIC ZONE
All Rights on behalf of itself and PAUL O'NEILL PUBLISHING Administered by WARNER-TAMERLANE PUBLISHING CORP.
All Rights Reserved

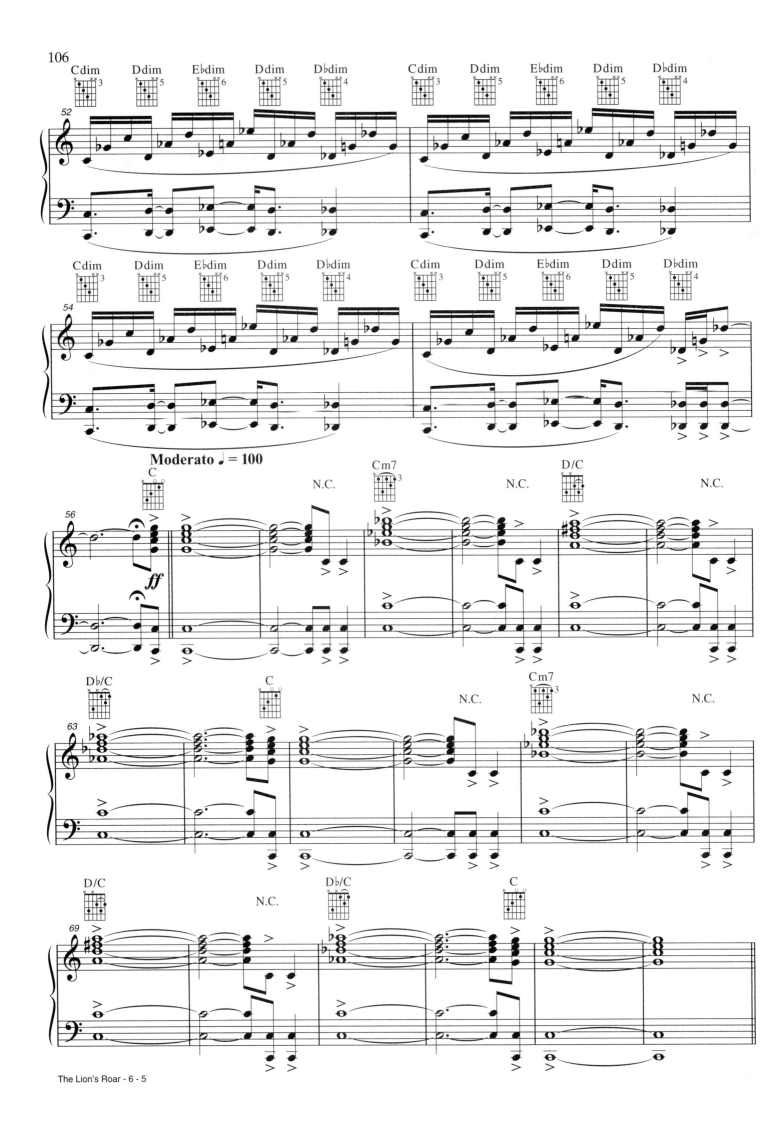

DREAMS WE CONCEIVE

Lyrics by
PAUL O'NEILL

Music by
PAUL O'NEILL and JOHN OLIVA

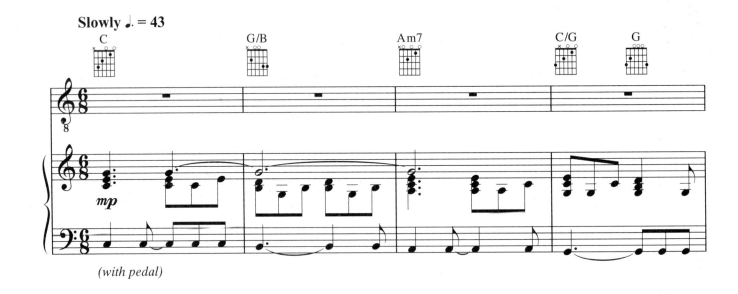

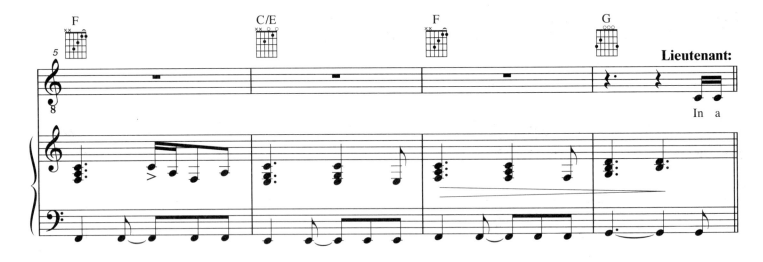

Dreams We Conceive - 9 - 1

© 2009 WARNER-TAMERLANE PUBLISHING CORP., PAUL O'NEILL PUBLISHING, WB MUSIC CORP. and JOHN OLIVA PUBLISHING DESIGNEE
All Rights on behalf of itself and PAUL O'NEILL PUBLISHING Administered by WARNER-TAMERLANE PUBLISHING CORP.
All Rights on behalf of itself and JOHN OLIVA PUBLISHING DESIGNEE Administered by WB MUSIC CORP.
All Rights Reserved

Dreams We Conceive - 9 - 9

126

There Was a Life - 17 - 10

MOONLIGHT AND MADNESS

Music by
PAUL O'NEILL and PAUL SILVERSTEIN

136

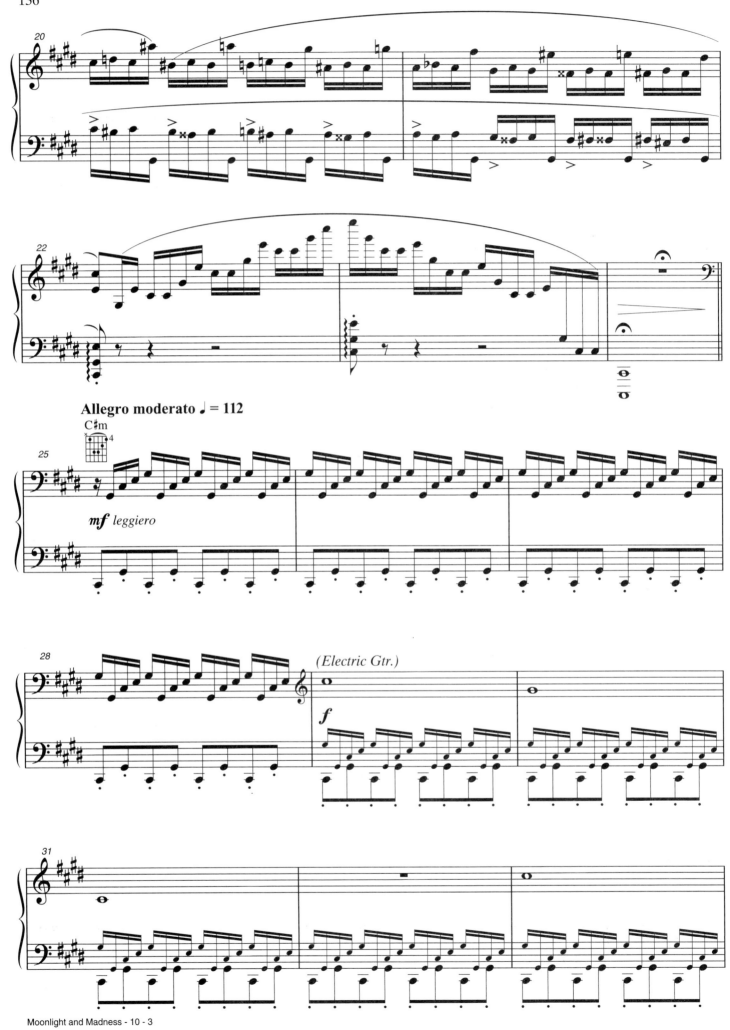

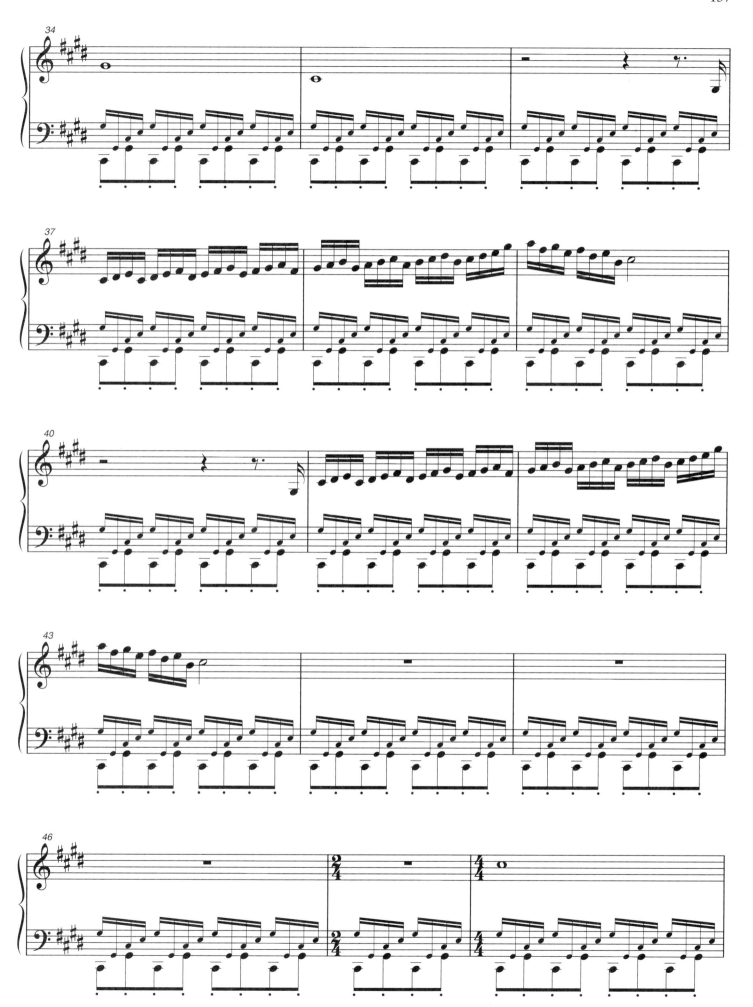

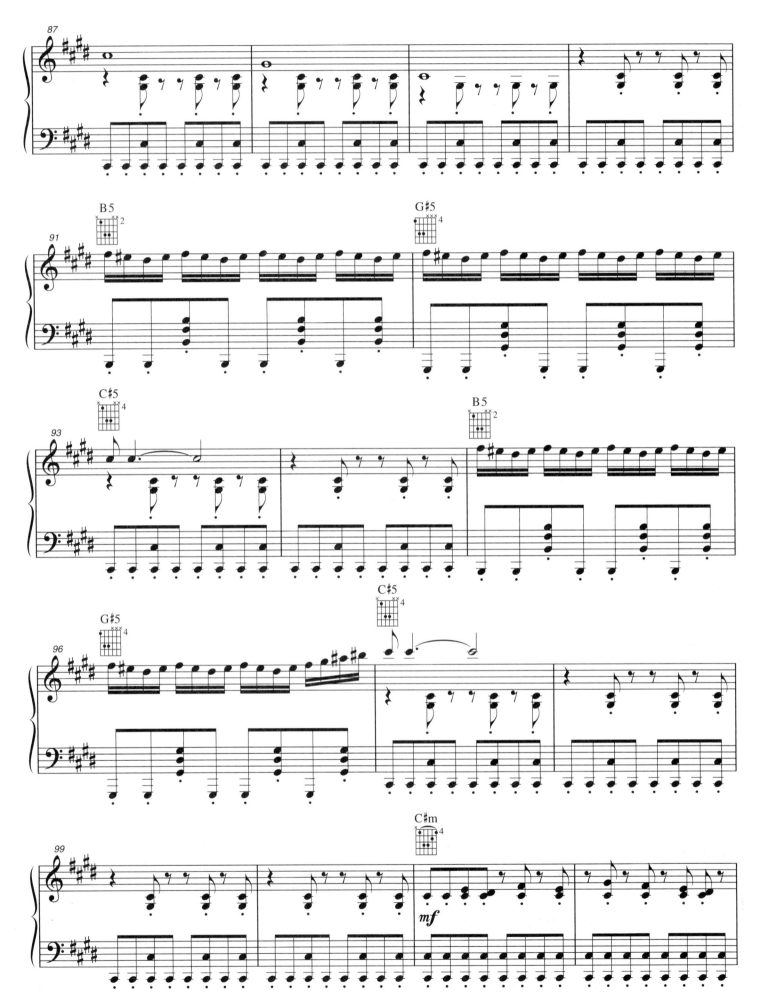

154

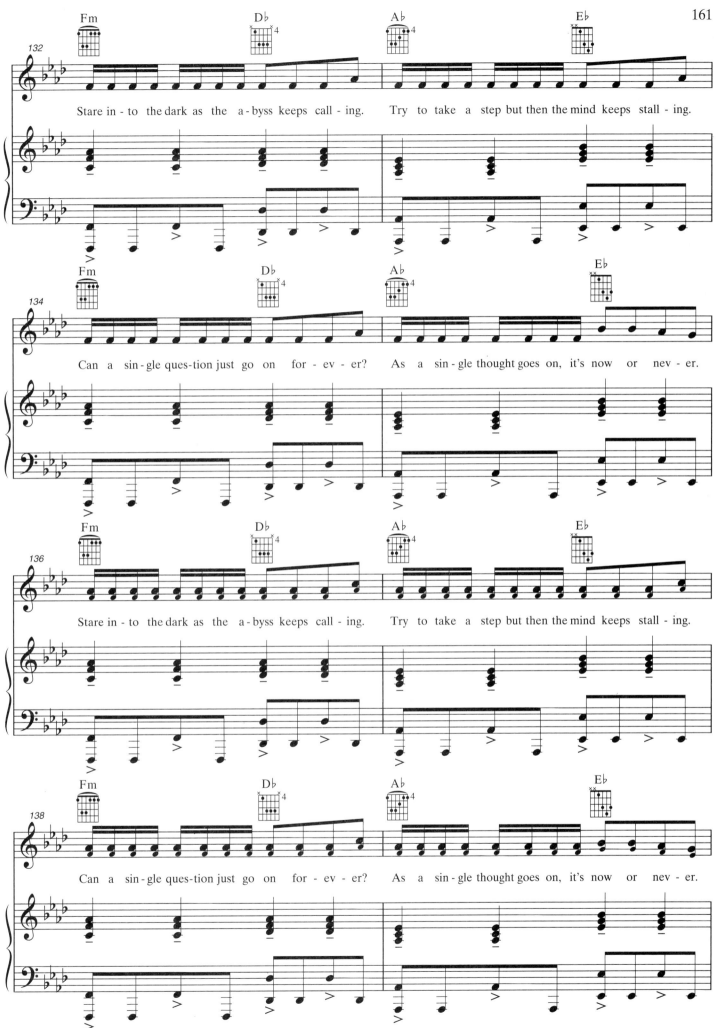

BACH LULLABY

Music by J.S. BACH
Arranged by PAUL O'NEILL

Father, Son and Holy Ghost - 12 - 11

REMNANTS OF A LULLABY

EMBERS

Gtr. tuned G6 tuning.
⑥ = D   ③ = G
⑤ = G   ② = B
④ = D   ① = E

Music by
PAUL O'NEILL

Moderato ♩ = 78

CHILD OF THE NIGHT

Lyrics by
PAUL O'NEILL

Music by
LEO DELIBES and PAUL O'NEILL

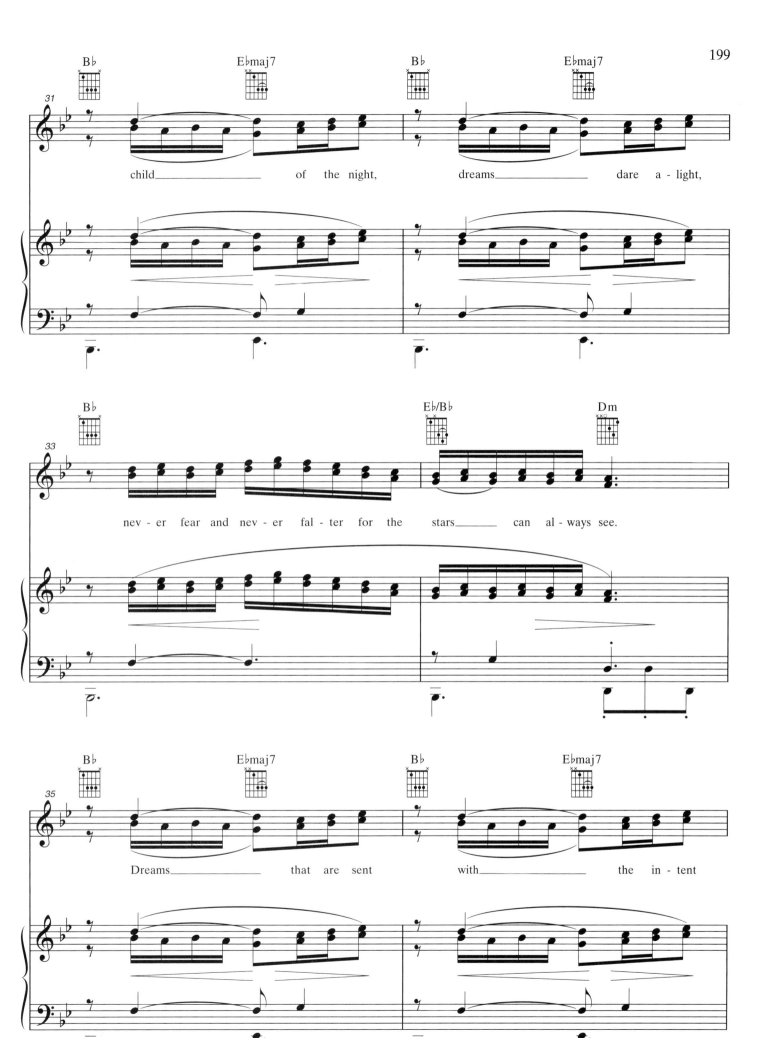

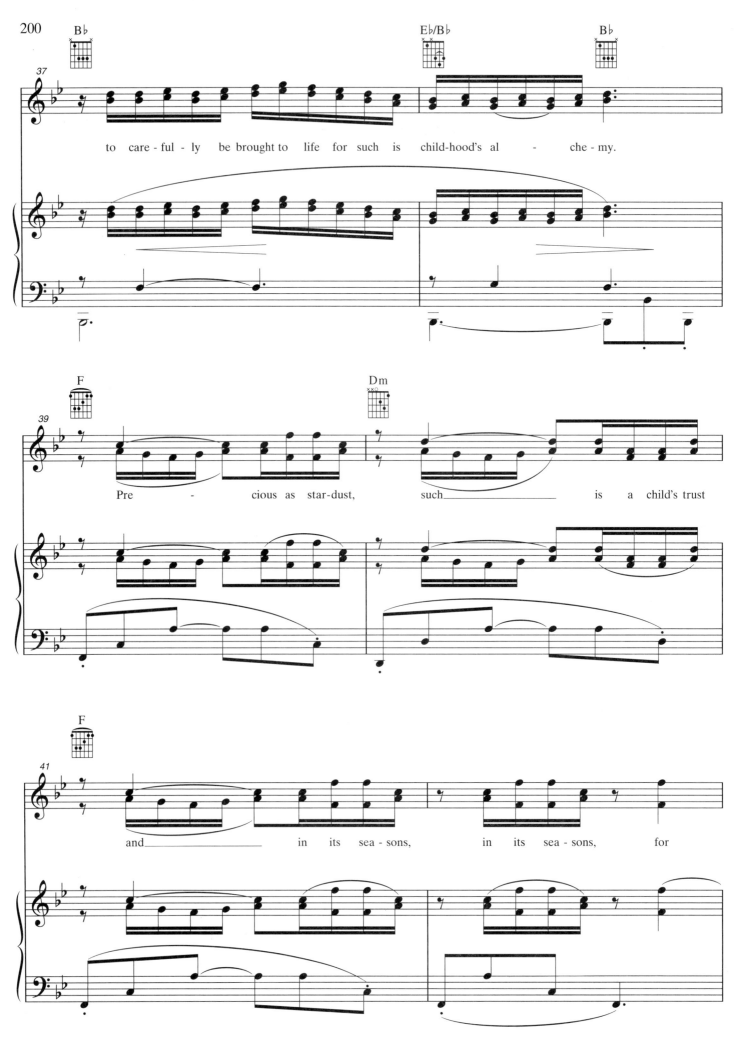

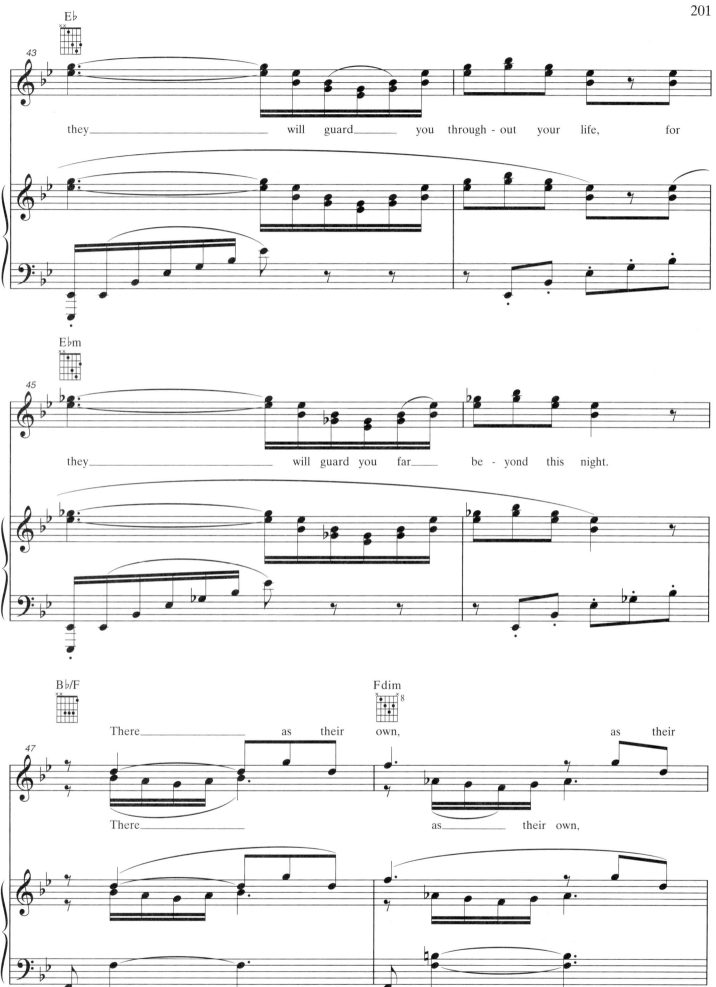

NUTROCKER

By KIM FOWLEY

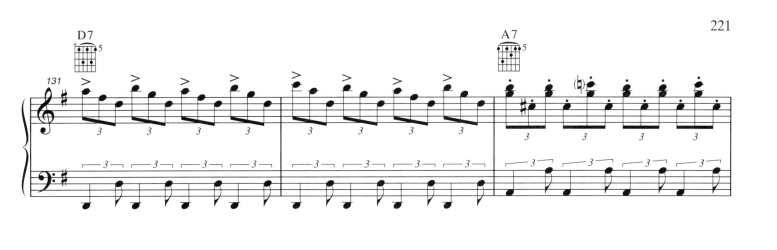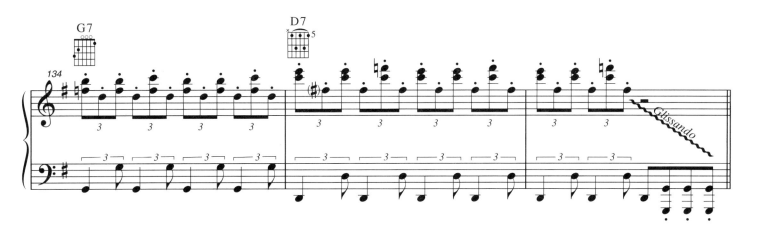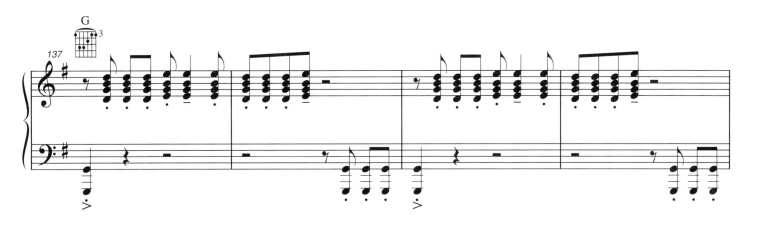

CARMINA BURANA

By CARL ORFF

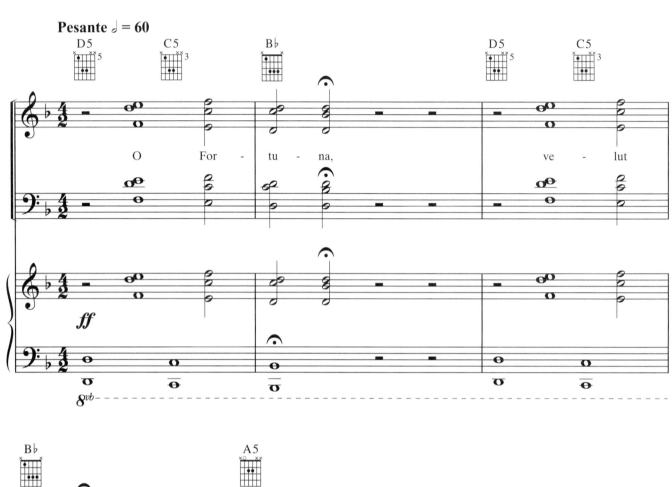

TRACERS

231

Lyrics by
PAUL O'NEILL

Music by
PAUL O'NEILL, AL PITRELLI
and JANE MANGINI

Allegro con fuoco ♩. = 127

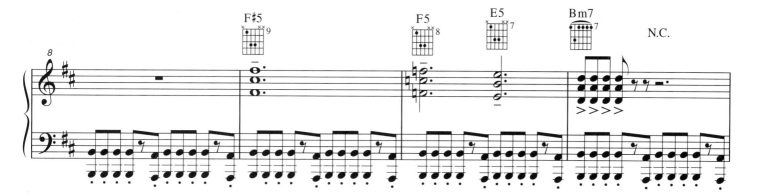

Tracers - 10 - 1

© 2009 WARNER-TAMERLANE PUBLISHING CORP., PAUL O'NEILL PUBLISHING, MIGHTY MUSIC ZONE and COPYRIGHT CONTROL
All Rights on behalf of itself and PAUL O'NEILL PUBLISHING Administered by WARNER-TAMERLANE PUBLISHING CORP.
All Rights Reserved